MW01201691

Come FLY wi

Poetry from A to Z

By Shayna Bresnick

Copyright © 2022 by Shayna Bresnick
Illustrations by Alexandra Rusu

All rights reserved. No part of this publication may be reproduced, distributed or
transmitted in any form or by any means, including photocopying, recording or other
electronic or mechanical methods, without the prior written permission of the publisher,
except in the case of brief quotations embodied in reviews and certain other non-
commercial uses permitted by copyright law.

This book is a work of fiction. Names, characters, places and incidents are either the
product of the author's imagination or are used fictitiously, and any resemblance to
actual persons, living or dead, events, or locales is entirely coincidental.

Printed in the United States of America

Print ISBN: 978-1-956019-03-2
eBook ISBN: 978-1-956019-04-9

Library of Congress Control Number: 2022904650

Published by DartFrog Plus, the hybrid publishing imprint of DartFrog Books.

Publisher Information:
DartFrog Books
4697 Main Street
Manchester, VT 05255
www.DartFrogBooks.com

*I dedicate this book to the courageous children
around the world battling cancer.*

*I would like to thank my wonderful family
and DartFrog publishing
for helping me publish this book.*

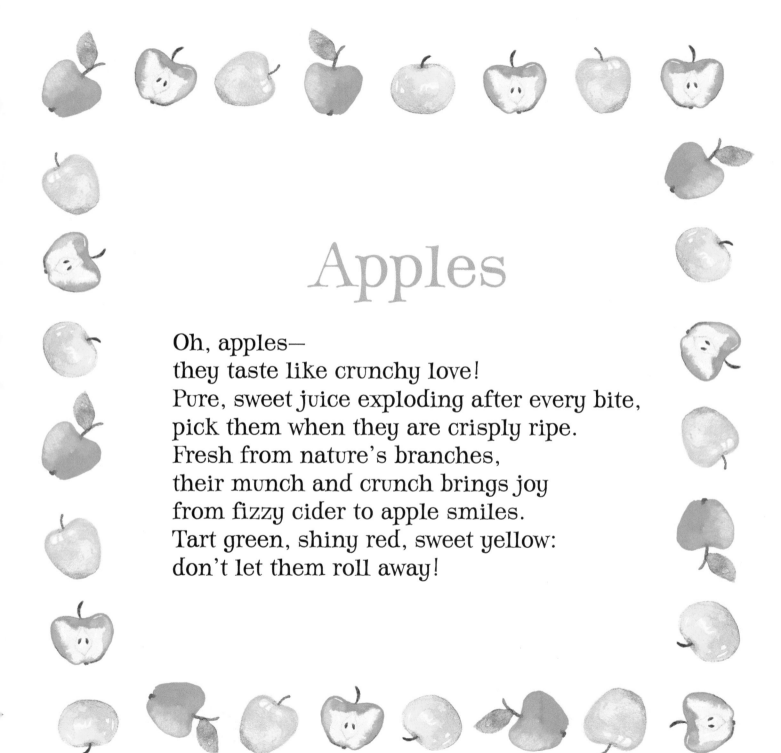

Apples

Oh, apples—
they taste like crunchy love!
Pure, sweet juice exploding after every bite,
pick them when they are crisply ripe.
Fresh from nature's branches,
their munch and crunch brings joy
from fizzy cider to apple smiles.
Tart green, shiny red, sweet yellow:
don't let them roll away!

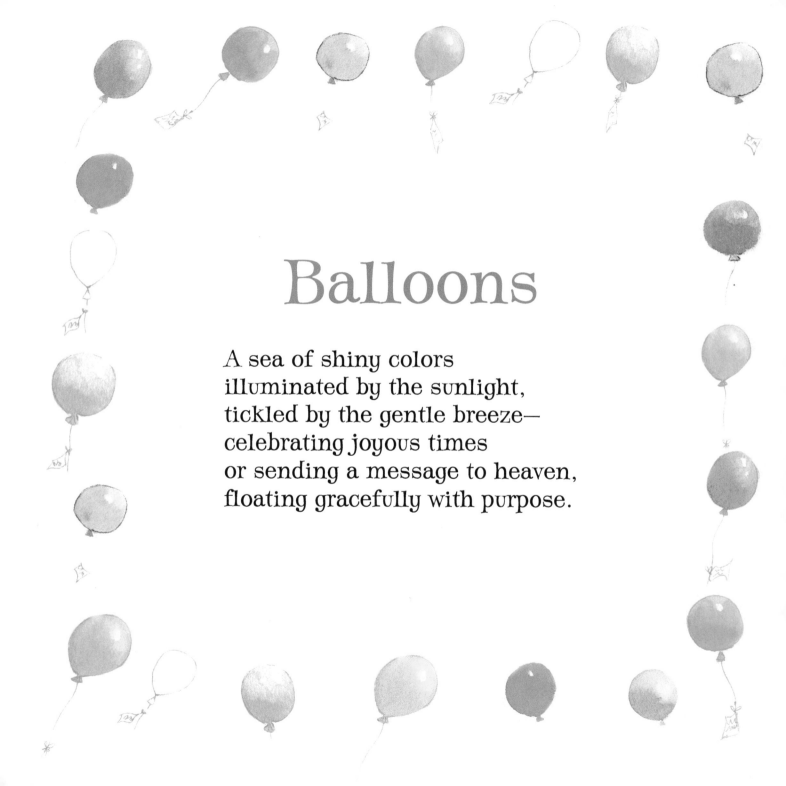

Balloons

A sea of shiny colors
illuminated by the sunlight,
tickled by the gentle breeze—
celebrating joyous times
or sending a message to heaven,
floating gracefully with purpose.

Catastrophes

If there is one letter in a poem that starts with C,
please use the word *catastrophe*!
Broken vases from baseball bats,
squirrels chasing cats,
doorbells that don't go "ding,"
birds that don't have wings—
what if a bird had no wings?
It would hop around kicking random things!
A chair with no legs,
a pirate's leg with no peg—
if everything was a catastrophe
then nothing would be normal, you see.

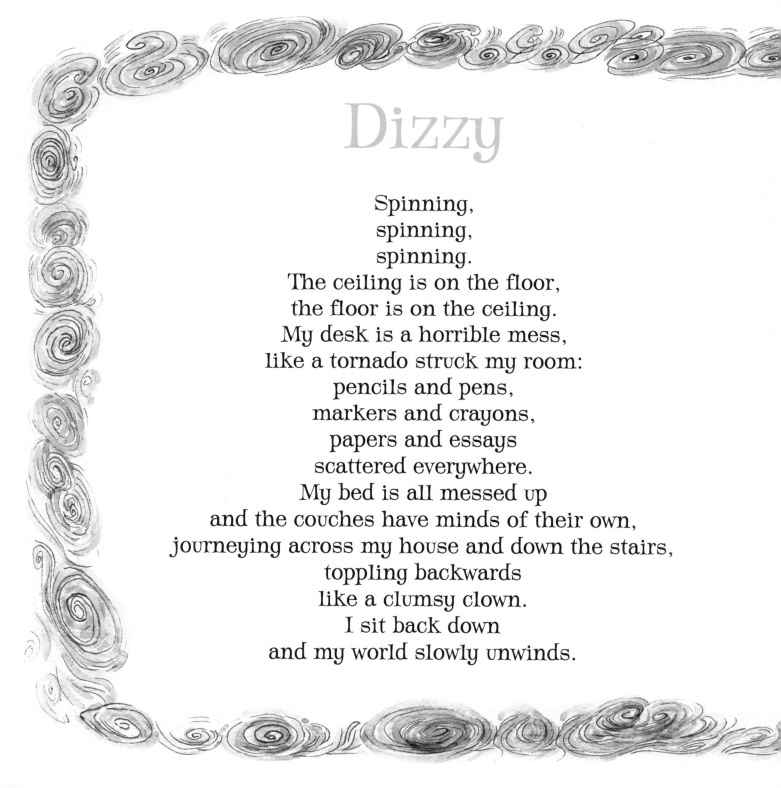

Dizzy

Spinning,
spinning,
spinning.
The ceiling is on the floor,
the floor is on the ceiling.
My desk is a horrible mess,
like a tornado struck my room:
pencils and pens,
markers and crayons,
papers and essays
scattered everywhere.
My bed is all messed up
and the couches have minds of their own,
journeying across my house and down the stairs,
toppling backwards
like a clumsy clown.
I sit back down
and my world slowly unwinds.

Eye Haiku

Blue, brown, green, grey, black
flecked with colors of the sea,
gazing at the world.

Freckles

Suzie Sarah really wants freckles:
freckles on her face,
not in the most embarrassing place!
All of her friends have them
and she wants them too.
Suzie Sarah says they'll make her look cute,
her parents say to be herself.
But wait!
What's that on her face?
She smiled when she saw her first freckle.

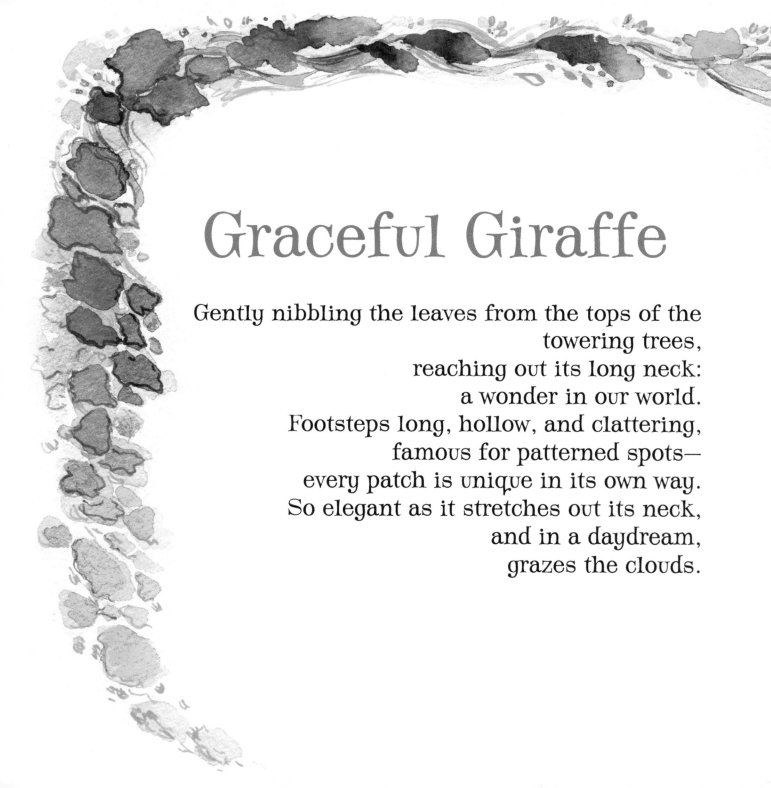

Graceful Giraffe

Gently nibbling the leaves from the tops of the
towering trees,
reaching out its long neck:
a wonder in our world.
Footsteps long, hollow, and clattering,
famous for patterned spots—
every patch is unique in its own way.
So elegant as it stretches out its neck,
and in a daydream,
grazes the clouds.

Hope

When you are hopeful, you might pray or pine for mercy.
You can have tears streaming down your cheeks,
or be jumping for joy.
You may feel anxiety,
or sadness,
or maybe a mix of the two.
You may scream,
or cry,
or think silently in your head.
You could be drawing,
or reading,
or listening to your favorite song.
You could be at school
or at home in your cozy bed,
snuggling closely with your stuffed little bear named Ted.
If you can dream,
you can hope—
even skiing on a slope!
Hope can be small and weak,
lacking confidence,
or mighty and fierce like a lion.
Never lose hope.

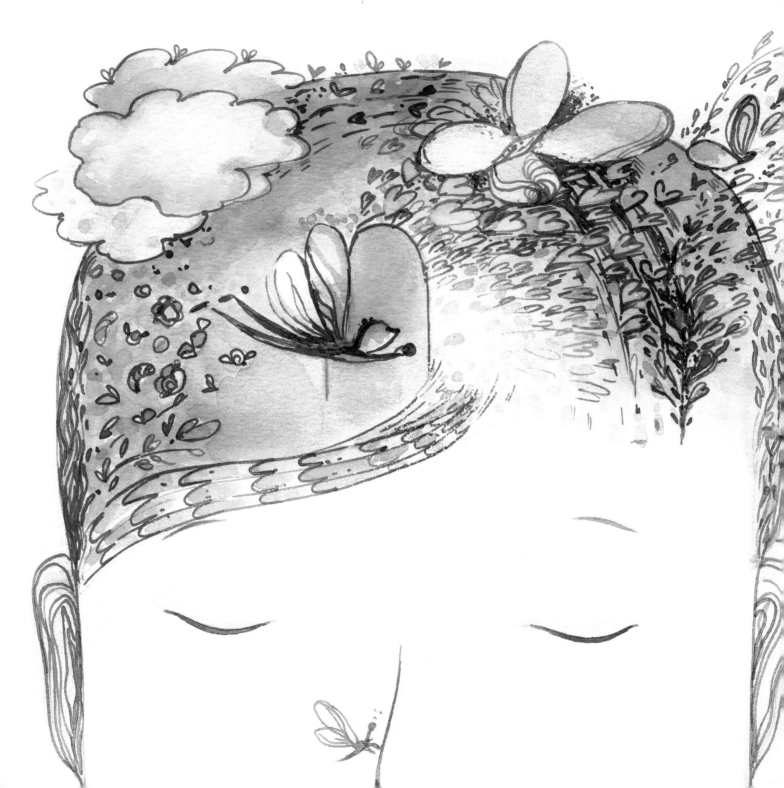

Imagination in Senses

Using your imagination can be so much fun!
If you use your senses—
hearing, smelling, touching, seeing, and tasting
there will be no time to waste
before you'll hear the deep rumbling roar of fire-breathing dragons
and the soft clicking of a unicorn's hoofs on the ground.
Trees and plants will speak our language
and nobody will ever yell or fight.
You can smell the sweetest smells
with a hint of roses mixed inside.
You can touch the softest things,
softer than the blanket given to a newborn baby.
You can see a world made of candy,
with lollipops as flowers and gumdrops as morning dew.
You can taste the scrumptious flavor of a food not yet invented,
or the freshest fruit picked off a tree.
The possibilities are endless
with senses and imagination!

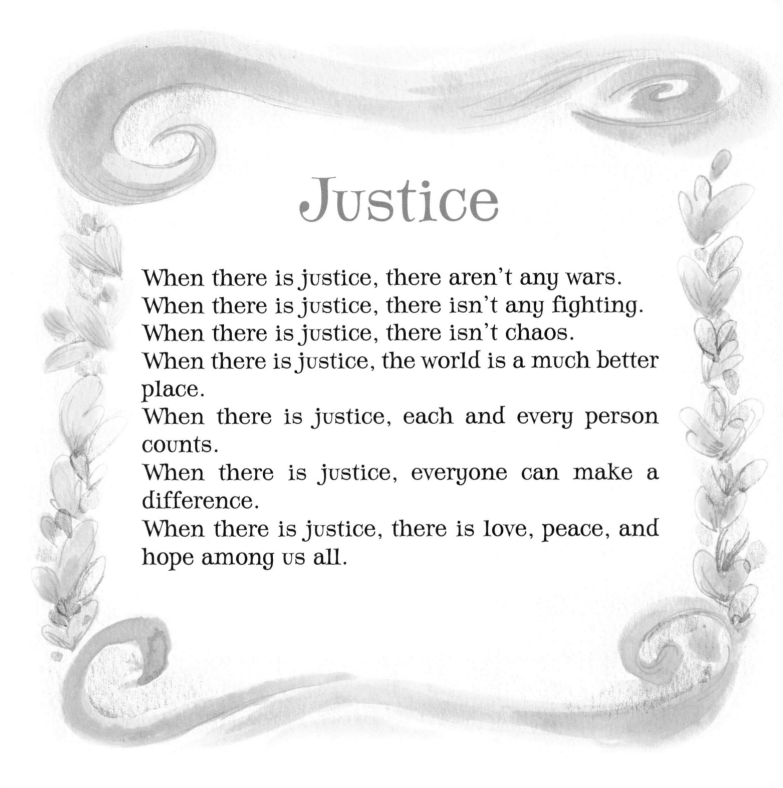

Justice

When there is justice, there aren't any wars.
When there is justice, there isn't any fighting.
When there is justice, there isn't chaos.
When there is justice, the world is a much better place.
When there is justice, each and every person counts.
When there is justice, everyone can make a difference.
When there is justice, there is love, peace, and hope among us all.

Knights

Working for the king: loyal.
Shining metal armor,
the heavy weight of defense: noble.
Their swords in use to protect,
clanging, crashing: unity.
Deafening sounds,
adversaries on the ground: powerful.
Losing many of their own men,
riding their galloping horses: gallant.
Overcoming the enemy,
their armor flashes in the moonlight: dignified.
They return to the castle,
forever working to protect their kingdom: loyal.

Love Is...

Love is a diamond
sparkling in the sunlight,
casting out a rainbow refraction.
Its value is so rare it is priceless.
Love is a photo hanging up on the wall,
its memories captured in time.
Love is a wooden table,
sturdy, polished, hard,
and each fiber is a developed friendship promised to last a
lifetime.
Love is a bouquet of roses,
so red and beautiful—
their petals grow and flourish just as love does.
Love is a piano,
and its enchanted sounds soothe my ears
as the keys are gently tickled
and it laughs an affectionate giggle.
Love is a white sheet of paper,
starting everything over with forgiveness and a clean slate.

My Family's Warmth

In his house, they never used lights.
The sun brightened their days
as it shone through the windows,
welcoming fresh, pure air.
In her house, they never had a television.
Her youngest brother was the comedian of the family,
bringing laughter and joy
day after day.
In my house, we had no heater.
Our family's love and happiness warmed us
as we huddled together in the cold winter.

Nocturnal Animals

The sun sets,
a curtain is drawn tight.
Peaceful relaxation,
then my sudden realization—
so much action
under the moonlight.
The stars shine bright,
illuminating us
like nature's night-light.
Eyes blink awake;
creatures, the night is yours!
Do the jobs that must be done,
nourish yourselves with food,
quench your thirst,
then doze again,
peacefully, quietly—
asleep when we arise.

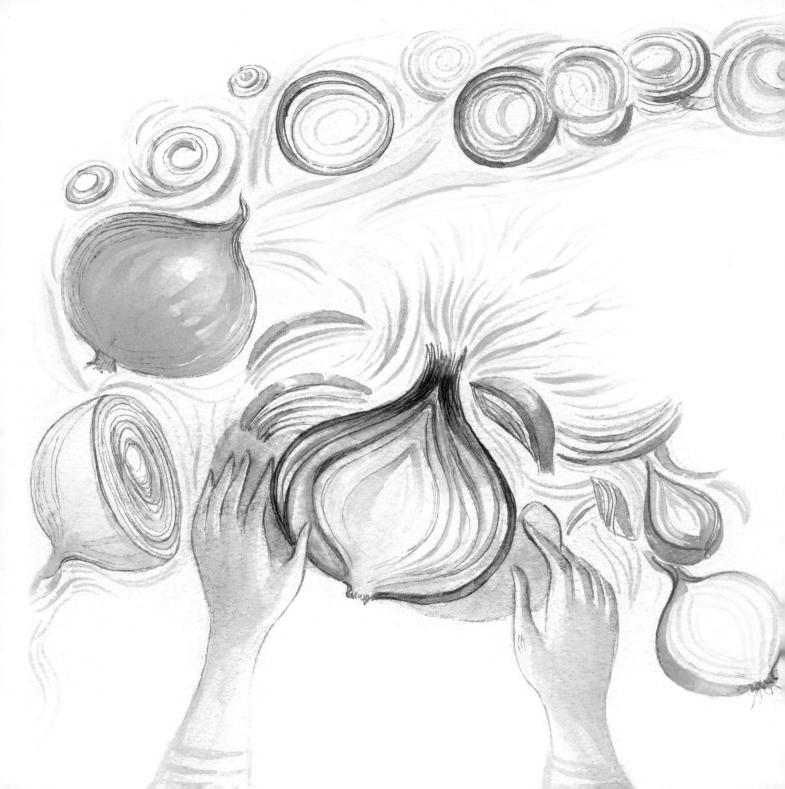

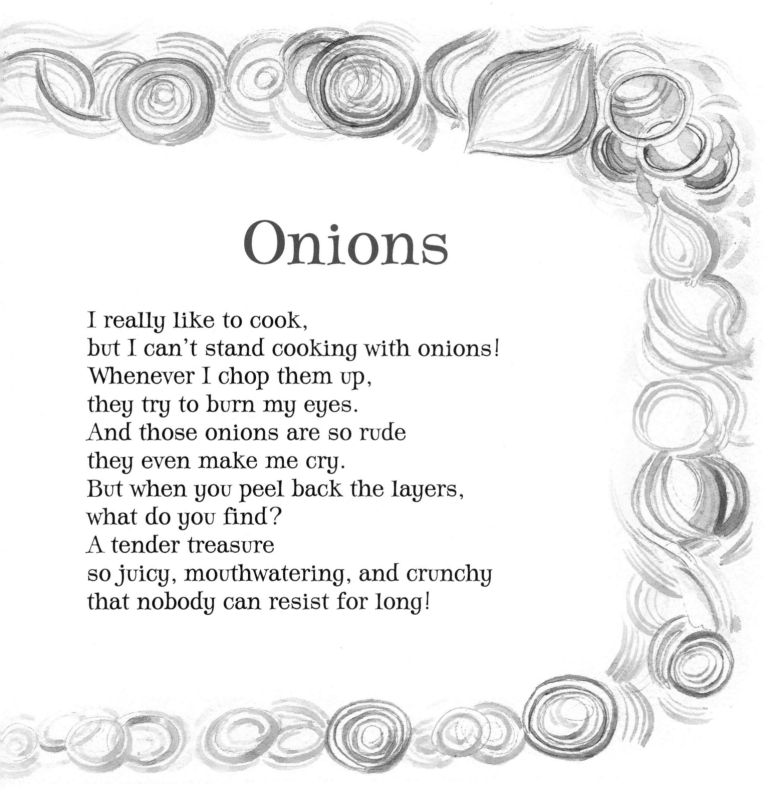

Onions

I really like to cook,
but I can't stand cooking with onions!
Whenever I chop them up,
they try to burn my eyes.
And those onions are so rude
they even make me cry.
But when you peel back the layers,
what do you find?
A tender treasure
so juicy, mouthwatering, and crunchy
that nobody can resist for long!

Packed Clothes

We don't like to be packed,
shoved and smooshed together
until we have no space.
We beg to leave,
but no one can hear us;
our voices are so small and squeaky.
We are tossed around,
dirty, cramped, and squeezed.
We wish we could run away.
Please treat us with care,
and you will never go bare.

Quivering

A cold winter night,
a quivering winter fright
sits with us by the stone fireplace.
Queer little shadows,
doors creaking,
a minuscule mouse squeaking.
The queen of the witches cackling,
her cauldron filled with nasty sights.
The werewolves howling at the moon,
their teeth as sharp as knives.
Dreaming while the fire keeps crackling,
I'm not even close to tackling
that eerie, quivering fear of winter frights.

Rewinding My Life

I've been living a very long life;
I'm about ninety-seven years old
and I want to rewind my life.
I need a chance to feel bold!
I need to make a time machine,
but that may be too hard;
you can't whittle one with a knife.
I guess it's not right.
We weren't meant to do this.
Wait! Hold on!
Imagining my past won't create a fight.
I could fly a rocket to years before now,
when I was young.
And I know how—
oh, yes!
I could hang from the monkey bars,
and from there I could climb my favorite oak tree.
I could also see myself as a baby
and hear my parents' strong voices giving me lectures,
but never screaming or yelling at me.
You see,
making a time machine with pure creativity isn't all that hard.

Sailboat

Once I had a little sailboat,
and she could really sail.
She persevered and even sailed through hail!
My sailboat was so small, but she had so much
might.
Once the sun came up, she could really fight.
But during the night, surrounded by the unknown,
she quivered quietly from fright.

Tears

What was once a handwoven basket filled with joy
is now one filled with salty tears that weigh upon my back.
The plants were growing,
the water was flowing,
and the flowers were blooming,
but my tears flooded them all.
Now a wound lives in my heart,
scarring me.
You can never glue the gash back together;
it almost sliced me in half,
cut me into pieces.
The worry for you,
the stressful times,
the shock makes me freeze like stone.
The news,
the blues,
the call from heaven.
I'll always cherish the memories of you,
and they will remain deep in my heart
forever.

Upside Down

I am hanging upside down,
my cat is dozing off on clouds
drifting across the floor.
The potted plants are defying gravity,
the sky is green like the grass,
and you are walking upside down too.

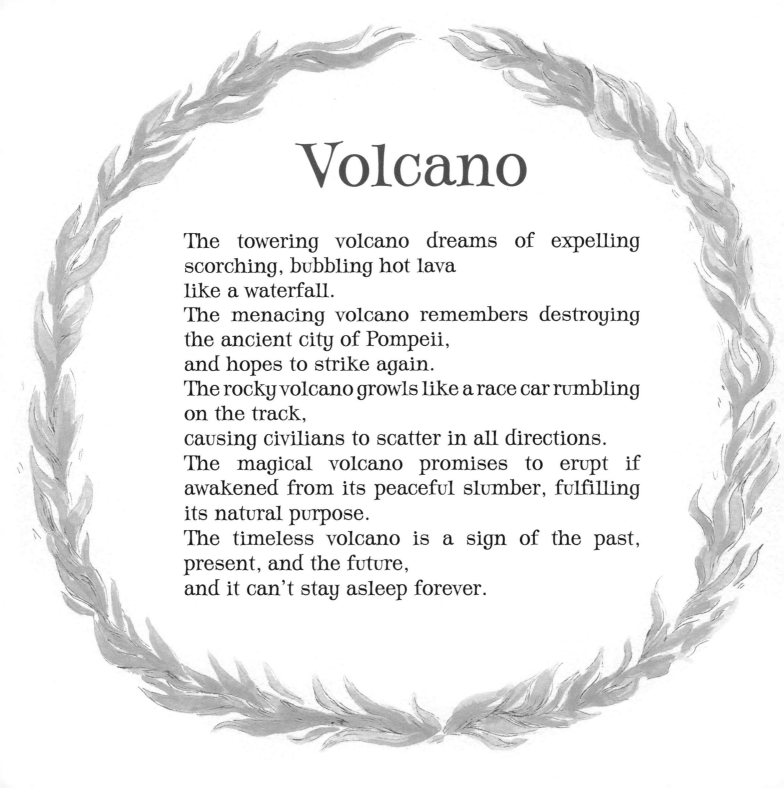

Volcano

The towering volcano dreams of expelling scorching, bubbling hot lava
like a waterfall.
The menacing volcano remembers destroying the ancient city of Pompeii,
and hopes to strike again.
The rocky volcano growls like a race car rumbling on the track,
causing civilians to scatter in all directions.
The magical volcano promises to erupt if awakened from its peaceful slumber, fulfilling its natural purpose.
The timeless volcano is a sign of the past, present, and the future,
and it can't stay asleep forever.

Waste

In the garbage can there is waste,
rotten fruits and oozing paste,
and a shoe with a hole
in its sole.
Boy, things can get out of control!
Parts of a tower
and a broken shower,
a laundry rag,
a plastic bag,
a missing key,
a little wooden tiki—
there is so much waste.
To keep the earth happy,
try to always recycle!

X-hale

Inhale,
x-hale.
Inhale,
x-hale.
Ahhhhhhh, so relaxing.
I finally found a way to get rid of
stress;
I feel warm, safe, and content,
stress-free like the summer sun,
peaceful like flowing, clear water.
Relaxation opens me up to a better
world,
dreams can take me anywhere.
Inhale,
x-hale.
Inhale,
x-hale.

Yum, Desserts!

The luscious brownie oozes chocolaty goodness,
soft, steaming, fresh from the oven
and on to my plate.
The bright, rainbow-colored sprinkles make me smile.
My heavenly-smelling cinnamon-apple pie
is topped with a scoop of delicious vanilla ice cream—
every bite bursts with fruity flavor.
I pull out my chair, relax, and enjoy!
My éclair is filled with sweet whipped custard
as airy as clouds in the sky.
Drizzled with warm chocolate that melts in my mouth,
it's perfect for my sweet tooth.
Vanilla ice cream: cold, sugary, and refreshing.
Mouthwatering sauces: hot fudge, vanilla, caramel,
and raspberry.
With a vibrant red cherry on top,
my sundae is perfect on a summer day.

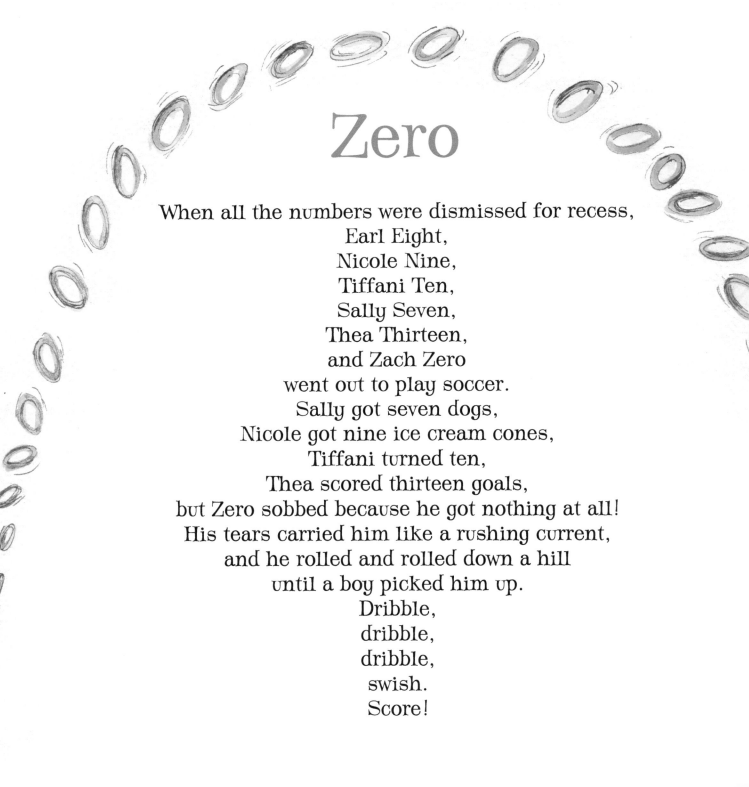

Zero

When all the numbers were dismissed for recess,
Earl Eight,
Nicole Nine,
Tiffani Ten,
Sally Seven,
Thea Thirteen,
and Zach Zero
went out to play soccer.
Sally got seven dogs,
Nicole got nine ice cream cones,
Tiffani turned ten,
Thea scored thirteen goals,
but Zero sobbed because he got nothing at all!
His tears carried him like a rushing current,
and he rolled and rolled down a hill
until a boy picked him up.
Dribble,
dribble,
dribble,
swish.
Score!

About the Author

Shayna Bresnick enjoys writing poetry and sharing her creations with others. Her poems have been featured in *A Celebration of Poets*, *Accomplished*, and *Skipping Stones* magazine.

Inspired to create a book for children following the loss of a family friend to cancer, Shayna began writing the poems for *Come Fly With Me: Poetry From A to Z* at the age of ten. She then decided to dedicate her efforts to helping raise funds for cancer research and care.

Shayna lives in Los Angeles, California, holds a black belt in Tae Kwon Do, and loves writing. When she's not creating poetry, Shayna enjoys going to the beach, spending time with friends and family, and volunteering as a teen mental health counselor.

What does an author stand to gain by asking for reader feedback? A lot. In fact, it's so important in the publishing world that they've coined a catchy name for it: "social proof." And without social proof, an author may as well be invisible in this age of digital media sharing.

So if you've enjoyed *Come Fly with Me: Poetry from A to Z*, please consider giving it some visibility by reviewing it on the sales platform of your choice. Your honest opinion could help potential readers decide whether or not they would enjoy this book, too.

CPSIA information can be obtained
at www.ICGtesting.com
Printed in the USA
BVHW061557160323
660603BV00017B/720

9 781956 019032